Shadows and

Anna Woods

BookLeaf
Publishing

Presentation by *BookLeaf Publishing*

Web: www.bookleafpub.com

E-mail: info@bookleafpub.com

ISBN: 9789357748490

First edition 2023

To the Man of my heart, no name needed you know who you are. I wrote most of these poems about you and we both know you helped me put it together. I love you Darling.

ACKNOWLEDGEMENT

Thank you to my Mother for teaching me to be a woman full of selfless love. To my Grandfather for passing down the gift of poetry and to my Father for being a man of deep emotion that taught me about strong relational values.

PREFACE

This poetry is sacred to me. Not necessarily due to its content, though that is sacred too, but because of the function that poetry itself has played in my life. I have written since I was a child. I began doing so shortly after the death of my Grandfather and since that time my poetry has been a source of relief for me. It flows from my soul like tears or laughter and at certain moments it has been a bloodletting of sorts. This particular collection is a snapshot of romantic relationships, the passion and heartbreak alike, some I have experienced and others I have imagined, but all an exhaled breath of the soul's desire to love and be loved in return.

I hope that you enjoy the perspective of him/her voices and that you find common ground that lives within the Shadows and Flame of us all.

Flame (Him)

I don't think they believe me
When I say my soul is a flame
They want to play with the fire
But it's always me they blame
I fall too hard I feel too much
It's fun and games until they touch
Burned they pull away
And I'm left here longing
For someone who remains
To dance within the Flame.

Hide Away (Her)

There's an ocean in your eyes
You don't even know it's there
A passion in your soul
But you act like you don't care
There's a kindness in your smile
Though you rarely let it out
There's a goodness in your heart
But your head is full of doubt
There's a softness in your touch
A love you hide away
Thinking no one knows the games you like to
play
There's a whispering of promise, a flickering of
light
A secret you won't tell, but I hear it in the night
You can play the fool, be silent if you must
You can break my heart, you can break my trust
But I still know the truth and it still sets me free
I believe in you
So, have some faith in me.

Golden Song (Him)

So many things inside of me may never see the
light.
Doubt and fear and reverie and tears that fall at
night,
But even if you never know the anguish I have
felt,
Your hands have soothed the soul in me and
made my heart feel held.

Every time you look at me, I am truly seen
And the knowledge that you care for me is such
a precious thing.
I won't take for granted all you are to me,
I'll treasure you like Golden Song and let you
help me sing.

The Leap (Her)

Touch me like a dainty flower
Cool me like a morning shower
Love me like the raging river flows
Free me from this cage of hatred
Make me glad that I have waited
Fill me full of all there is to know
See me standing on the edges
Of a cliff with rocky ledges
Falling now would be the death of me
But standing here makes me feel empty
And I long to jump off quickly
Thinking maybe then I would be free
And wondering if you'd catch me

Need (Him)

I just need days in your presence and nights in
your arms.
Moments where all I can see
Are your eyes
And all I can feel
Are your lips on mine.
I just need time!
To soak you up and breathe you in
To touch and taste and know your skin.
I need to absorb your wisdom
And to be consumed by who you are.
I need your heart!

Crave (Him)

It's crazy how I crave you
And I guess I wouldn't blame you
If my intensity made you question my sanity.
But truth be told I cannot hold all this love
inside of me.
It tumbled out without a doubt
And you became the flame that burns me inside
out.

Calling the Wind (Her)

It's amazing how you play me
Like a fine guitar
Like a flute or piano
Straight from the heart

It's as if I'm the music
And you know every note
Music without words
A melody you wrote

A song about forever
The endless dream of love
You call it from my soul
Like the heavens call a dove

And I must take its wings
And soar with you again
Carried on the melody
You wrote to call the wind

I Want You (Him)

I want you
To be the soft place I land
When the world is too much
I want to know your hand
Is beneath my head and around my heart
I want you to be where I am
Where I end
And the place I start

Promise (Her)

Promise me roses
Promise me dreams
Talk to me in riddles
Tell me what they mean

Share with me your secrets
Tell me all your fears
Let me know you love me
Cast on me your cares

Trust me when we're older
Love me while we're young
Teach how to hold you
And every song you've ever sung

Let me learn to love you
Every single part
Let me shine my love into
The shadows of your heart

If (Him)

If I could travel anywhere
I would travel everywhere
I'd take you along, I'd write you a song
And I'd sing it to the sea
If I could choose just anyone
You would be my only one
We would dance in fields of heather
In any kind of weather
Free as the birds we would be
If I could make my dreams come true
Don't you know I'd marry you?
And Darling you would want to marry me
If I could hold you close to me
I'd never let you go from me
And in my arms, you'd always want to be.

Chemistry (Her)

You whispered in my ear, "What do you need"?
My soul crashed into you at full speed
You listened to my tales of past regret
And condemned those vagabonds of their petty
theft
You promised to show me how it should have
been
Then made love to me like the first time once
again
Soft and sweet your mouth upon my own
The flames inside me now are full grown
I clutch you to myself in desperate grasp
Then bite your razor jaw to hear you gasp
My fingertips caress your silken side
Skin to skin your eyes dive into mine
I reach the edge and tumble to the end
I've fallen and I can't begin again
To tell you how this even came to be
Such perfect strong and lovely chemistry.

Known (Them)

Please let me sing that I love you.
Let me give you what I can.
I see no one above you,
Knowing you're just a man.
Let me so often hold you
Till I know all your skin
And hear you speak freely time and again.
I don't mind if you're angry or frustrated with me,
As long as you kiss me when affection breaks free.
I just want to love you
And build with you here
In this world that's so jaded
And flooded with fear.
I don't want to change you
Or make you my own
I just want to hold you and let you be KNOWN.

Melting (Them)

I lie on my back and look into your face
guarded and closed like a wall with no gate.
Then your lips meet mine and it melts my mind,
the tenderest trace of something Devine.
You gentle your touch as you plunder and take,
your hands blazing trails leaving chills in their
wake.
This lusty desire that pulls us in, driving us
higher skin to skin.
There are flames inside
Your lovely eyes
Whipped to a blaze by my sultry sighs
I'm melted like wax as we rise and fall
The walls coming down, you give me your all
Again, I am taken by all that you are
A universe spinning contained in a heart.

Man of my Heart (Her)

You have no idea how much I adore you
With your purple eyes and your fairy hair
The way you flash and glow and light up a room
The simple way everything you do has flair

The way your sunset smile can dim the world,
and make Hollywood tame to your wild
Like a warped record or a broken cassette
That doesn't play the tune just right
That's what the narrative of your life sounds like

You're a mess and it's wonderful
Your cadence is my favorite tune
With its pits and pockets
Your beauty blooms

And I see you for who you really are
Imperfect, but still the Man of my heart.

Lifetimes (Them)

I've lived lifetimes with you in my dreams
Decades and centuries of time
When I awake my heart just breaks
To find I'm once again confined
To the tiniest portion of a single day
To the minuscule moments of a passing night
Where you have politely asked me to stay
But I've lived lifetimes with you in my mind
There is a universe inside my soul
You're not its center, but you make it whole
And without your spinning miraculous mass
I think the rest would shatter like glass
How did I make it so many days
Without the fire you set ablaze
Before I felt your lovely touch
The whole of this world was not enough.

Remains (Them)

Our love was a rose in beautiful bloom
The essence of a lovely day
A fragile white blossom of truth and grace
That's not often found on the way
Until one night on a sob and a sigh
Its color was dreadfully changed
From the purest of whites to a deep crimson
stain
The color of blood and shame
With sorrow and lies and the flick of your wrist
The rose was tossed into the flames
Now the ashes of roses and the loss in my eyes
Is all of US that remains.

Silence (Him)

I have loved you Baby
Like a slow-moving train
Like the wild nights of Vegas
Like the calm days of Maine
I have found no peace in dreaming
I have found no love in war
I can't break through the silence
I'm not strong like before
Just behind the laughter
There's a heartache burning still
Just beyond the sunlight
There's a void that I can't fill
Somewhere in the darkness
There's something I must find
Somehow, I must reach you
Before I lose my mind

Design (Her)

I miss the way our bodies fit together,
Like puzzle pieces made to do the same.
Made to create a picture of what is and still
could be.

I love the curve of your back,
From shoulder blade to hip.
I let my fingertips graze your spine and nestle at
your neck as my lips kiss your chin.
Your hardness deep inside stroking my mind
with scintillating pleasures of true Devine
Design

Him (Her)

Oh to feel the cling of him,
The sting of him,
The sweet dark ring of him.

Oh to feel him breathe
To watch him spin
In, out, around and away
To call the coming day.

Rear View Mirror (Him)

As I gaze in the rearview mirror of my life
I see the red stain of my heart smeared across
the pavement
The bits and pieces of my soul swept into a pile
on the side of the road.
I have been roadkill too many times to count,
but you still can't count me out.
I will rise!
From the trauma and the massacre
I will again be made new
Fresh as morning rain I will fall on you.
I will bear my scars and I'll still live these
dreams
No matter what the past has been I am more than
what I seem

A Garden Dream (Them)

The sunlight danced across your face
And the wind played with your hair
Your smile became a silent laugh
And your eyes were warm and fair
The Gardens fragrant blossoms
Surrounded you and I
And you became my hero
With naught but just a sigh
Your voice was soft as velvet
And like a lover's touch
Caressing me with whispers
That would never be enough
And there in the evening sunlight
With your breath upon my skin
My heart reached out to take your hand
And welcome you within

Printed in the USA
CPSIA information can be obtained
at www.ICGtesting.com
CBHW071318200724
11858CB00024B/676